EVALUATING PRINCIPALS

Issues and Practices

James E. Green

Phi Delta Kappa Educational Foundation
Bloomington, Indiana U.S.A.

Cover design by
Victoria Voelker

Phi Delta Kappa Educational Foundation
408 North Union Street
Post Office Box 789
Bloomington, IN 47402-0789
U.S.A.

Printed in the United States of America

Library of Congress Control Number 2003099220
ISBN 0-87367-850-8

Table of Contents

Chapter 1

ISSUES IN THE EVALUATION OF PRINCIPALS

Leadership is an elusive concept. Attempts to evaluate leadership usually seem to miss the mark. Should we evaluate the leader's personal qualities? Or should we evaluate what the leader accomplishes, regardless of personality or leadership style? Most of us could answer "yes" to either question, only to find that either stance leads to more questions.

Evaluating leadership in schools is particularly perplexing because a principal must play many roles, such as master teacher, mentor, curriculum specialist, civic leader, business manager, disciplinarian, and role model to both pupils and professionals. Today's principal must balance a seesaw. On one end are stacked the needs and expectations of teachers, pupils, and parents; on the other, the needs and expectations of district administrators, the school board, and, by extension, state and federal governments. This balancing act is complicated by challenging socioeconomic conditions that affect students and their families in many communities, as well as by increasingly standards-driven expectations layered on by districts and states.

Another dimension of evaluation raises a new question: Who should be involved in evaluating a principal's leadership? Principals are accountable in some way to many constituents: students, parents, and teachers. All of these groups expect the principal to be a leader. In addition, the principal is directly accountable to the central office administrators. Most people would agree that all of these constituencies should be involved in a principal's evaluation.

Leadership also presents some paradoxes. For example, two principals may appear to have similar attributes and be equally skilled, yet one succeeds while the other fails. Conversely, two principals may be similarly successful but reveal very different strengths and weaknesses. Is there an all-encompassing model? And what about how others view the principal? Principals are supposed to be caring and compassionate, but they also must maintain high standards and hold pupils, teachers, and staff accountable. A quality that makes the principal effective in the eyes of some — decisiveness, for example — can be viewed by others as unwillingness to collaborate or compromise. No wonder we still are searching for the best way to evaluate school principals.

Five basic questions can serve as a framework for discussing the evaluation of school principals: What is the purpose of evaluation? Who should evaluate? What should we evaluate? What standards or criteria should we use? What evidence should we consider?

What Is the Purpose of Evaluation?

Formal evaluation of principals must serve an explicit purpose. Otherwise, why do it? Although many evaluation plans fail to state one or more purposes explicitly, researchers have identified several typical reasons to evaluate (Genova et al. 1976):

- Evaluating the attainment of institutional goals.
- Helping with the improvement of professional performance.
- Providing data for personnel decisions.
- Improving the effectiveness of an administrative team.
- Providing data for reassignment or retraining.
- Keeping a governing board informed of adherence to policy.
- Sharing governance.
- Keeping constituencies informed about administrator effectiveness.
- Conducting research on administrator effectiveness.

We evaluate principals for three reasons (Genova et al. 1976). First, district administrators need reliable information on which to base personnel decisions. Second, principals need reliable feedback to help them improve professional performance. And third, principals need reliable feedback to help them guide their professional development.

In designing a system of formal evaluation, we need to consider various stakeholders in the process. Principals seek to identify and pursue opportunities for professional growth. District administrators need some basis for retaining, re-assigning, promoting, and compensating principals. The school board demands data describing the alignment of priorities and goals at school and district levels. In addition, teachers, staff, and parents all need to feel as though their voices are being heard in the evaluation process. Consequently, asking the purpose of evaluation gives rise to another question: Who should evaluate?

Who Should Evaluate?

The question of who should evaluate principals strikes at the heart of how modern schools work. Schools are both bureaucracies and democracies. They are bureaucracies because they must operate according to the policies and procedures determined by a hierarchical organization of which they are a part. They are democracies because they represent and serve a political constituency — the neighborhood. In the middle of this obvious contradiction is the principal, who is responsible to both the school community and the district administration. Both will judge the principal, whether or not their explicit participation is invited.

Although most formal evaluation plans focus mainly on how a principal's supervisor evaluates the principal, creating a truly fair process means including all parties who have a stake in the principal's professional performance. Parents, students, teachers, and staff at the school site need to have a meaningful voice in the process.

What Should We Evaluate?

The first hurdle in evaluating leadership is to determine what matters: style or substance. Evaluating style leads us to consider which particular personal attributes we should value. Evaluating substance pushes us to determine which indicators we should observe.

The indicators we use are important. In a corporate board room, for example, substance usually is defined in such quantifiable terms as market share, revenue, profit, and equity value. If we followed this example, we would place the emphasis on standardized test scores when evaluating the substance of leadership. However, leadership in schools is much more than just raising test scores.

What we choose to measure is a key issue. In Chapter Two I will consider the objective basis of evaluation by analyzing the nature of leadership in school communities. Researchers have identified personal traits and professional skills associated with effective school leadership, and these need to be explicit target behaviors in any evaluation system. If we are to evaluate the person, then what we observe about that person needs to be informed by research.

In Chapter Three I take up the question of performance-based evaluation. Management by objectives (MBO) and other forms of goal-directed evaluation originated in business and are slowly making their way into education. The emphasis in performance-based evaluation is on results — what the principal accomplishes in terms of predetermined performance objectives. Instead of observing a principal's leadership style, we measure pupil achievement, monitor attendance rates, or count suspensions and expulsions. But someone, or some group, still must determine which objectives are worth pursuing and set performance expectations.

What Criteria Should We Use?

The most common tool for evaluating school administrators is a rating scale with criteria that have been prescribed by the school district (Green 2002). Typically, the form is adopted at the district level after an informal process involving school principals. Implicit in the use of district-level criteria is agreement between the district administrators (namely, the superintendent) and the school principals regarding the criteria to be used.

National standards provide an alternative to using criteria developed at the district level. The Interstate School Leaders Licensure Consortium, a project of the Council of Chief State School Officers, published *Standards for School Leaders* in 1996. ISLLC standards have been adopted in various forms by more than half the states for administrator training programs, giving them the advantage of wide exposure within the profession. Another set of criteria is available from the National Association of Elementary School Principals through *Leading in Learning Communities: Standards for What Principals Should Know and Be Able to Do* (2001).

One advantage of using national standards is the credibility that comes from a professional organization of school administrators. However, national standards often can be worded vaguely and not be helpful for observing actual performance. To be useful, criteria must have some basis for observation. In addition, they require a local context.

What Evidence Should We Consider?

Evidence is how we back up judgment. Because we are making judgments when we evaluate principals, evidence becomes a central issue in the evaluation system. Where do we find the evidence to decide whether a principal meets the criteria that have been established?

Why we evaluate, *who* should evaluate, and *what* we evaluate all determine the nature of the evidence to be used in an evaluation system. For example, if the purpose of the evaluation is to rank principals according to progress they make toward meeting standardized testing targets, then test score averages are valid evidence. If we decide that teachers should have a say in the evaluation of their principal, then data from a survey of teachers are necessary.

Whatever evidence we decide to use, whatever standards, and whatever purpose, three criteria should be applied to the evaluation process itself. Hoyt (1982) concluded that effective evaluation of administrators needs credibility, validity, and fairness.

Credibility. Everyone must believe in the process: the principals who are being evaluated, the teachers and staff who have input into the evaluation, and the supervising administrators who facilitate the evaluation. Otherwise the outcome will be of little use. Whether a group gives credence to the process seems to depend on whether that same group was allowed to make a meaningful contribution to the design of the process. Also, according to Razik and Swanson (1995) credibility depends on whether the evaluation has the potential to help those who are evaluated.

Validity. What the evaluator observes must be relevant to the criteria for the evaluation. For example, if one of the criteria indicates that the principal should involve teachers, staff, and parents in development and evaluation of school policies and procedures, then the evaluation must be grounded in evidence that these groups have, in fact, been represented. The more tangible the proof, the easier it is to determine the validity of an observation. In this case, valid evidence might include surveys of constituent groups or the minutes of school-site council meetings.

Fairness. The principal should know who participates in the evaluation process, how they are involved, and how the results will be used in subsequent personnel decisions. The evaluation should not hold a principal accountable for anything that is outside the scope of the principal's responsibilities or control (Razik and Swanson 1995). For example, if a year of contentious collective bargaining between the teachers union and the board of education results in a general strike, it probably is not fair to hold a principal responsible for low teacher morale.

Research on Administrator Evaluation

The methods used to evaluate principals should be guided by research. However, studies of the evaluation of administrators in elementary and secondary schools are scarce. Research on the evaluation of leadership comes mainly from organizational psychology, and only a few studies have focused on the evaluation of leaders of education organizations.

Hogan, Curphy, and Hogan (1994) identified five categories of studies on the evaluation of leadership, and their framework is helpful for gaining a perspective on ways that we might evaluate school administrators. The first category is the *performance of the organizational unit*. Measuring a principal's performance in terms of students' standardized test scores is an example of this category.

In the second category, *ratings by subordinates, peers, and supervisors* predominate. Nearly every administrator is familiar with this procedure. The district adopts a rating form that lists criteria accompanied by a Likert-type scale, then someone (or some group) rates the administrator. Usually the rating is done annually. Studies in this category view leadership as a function of how well the leader is perceived by constituents. Interestingly, subordinates and supervisors often agree on an administrator's overall performance while evaluating very different technical aspects of that performance (Hogan et al. 1994).

The third category identified by Hogan, Curphy, and Hogan focuses on the *assessment of leadership potential* through interviews, assessment centers, or some form of simulation. While helpful for selecting personnel for management positions, research suggests that these methods do not help to improve professional performance or guide professional growth of administrators. Howard and Bray (1990) found that these assessment activities are most useful for predicting a candidate's prospects for advancing within a particular organization's culture. They are not designed to evaluate actual job performance.

In the fourth category, *self-evaluation* is considered. However, Farr and Dobbins (1989) observed that self-assessment has little value beyond stimulating discussion in an evaluation conference. Even so, personal reflection through self-assessment is a condition of true professional growth (Green and Smyser 1996). As a consequence, administrator portfolios — a type of self-assessment — are finding increasing acceptance. Brown and Irby (1997) have described the administrator portfolio as an evaluation tool designed to promote personal reflection and professional growth.

The fifth category takes a very different slant by investigating *factors associated with negative performance*. According to Hogan and his colleagues (1994), incompetence is associated with the following factors: untrustworthiness, overcontrol, exploitation, micromanagement, irritability, unwillingness to use discipline, and inability to make good staffing decisions. While helpful for identifying behaviors that should be avoided, the research from organizational psychology in this category does not reveal the best practices for evaluating the performance of leaders when the purpose is improving performance or guiding professional growth.

The literature on evaluating leadership in schools mainly describes practices. Representative of this approach is Elio Zappulla's *Evaluating Administrative Performance: Current Trends and Practices* (1983), which, in spite of being 20 years old, continues to be an excellent resource for describing practices used in school districts. Similar but more recent studies (Stine 2001; Thomas et al. 2000) provide updates to Zapulla's work, though they reveal that very little has changed.

However, some new techniques are emerging. Brown and Irby (1997) have outlined the professional portfolio approach to administrator assessment. They stress the importance of personal reflection as part of the evaluation process. In addition, the use of peer evaluation has been introduced as a method for promoting more professional dialogue in the evaluation process (Gil 2001). Empowerment of school constituencies and the use of multiple sources of data have been the thrust of "360-degree feedback" (Dyer 2001). Finally, management by objectives (MBO) includes a performance review dimension, though Razik and Swanson (1995) report that MBO as performance evaluation has achieved mixed results.

Even though we know that the principal is the key to a school's success, we have done little to help principals get better. Many principals report that the procedures used to evaluate them are helpful neither for improving their professional performance nor for guiding their future professional growth. Where this is the case, we need new strategies for evaluating principals, strategies that have credibility with principals, make use of valid evidence, and are fair.

Chapter 2

QUALITIES OF EFFECTIVE PRINCIPALS

James McGregor Burns (1978) discussed the difficulty of explaining what effective leaders actually do and the personal qualities that they possess. He observed that leadership is enigmatic by nature. We know an effective principal when we see one at work, but we have trouble coming up with a unifying theory of leadership in schools. We can recognize personal attributes and professional skills that are common among highly effective leaders, but these attributes *by themselves* are no guarantee of success.

While researchers continue to struggle over a unified theory of leadership, in practice superintendents still are responsible for evaluating principals. We need to take what we do know about leadership in schools and use that knowledge in our evaluation systems. The evaluation of principals must be grounded in what we know about the qualities of effective principals — what they do and the kind of people they are. A profile of effective leadership in school settings, incomplete though it may be, can be helpful in working toward improved evaluation. In this chapter I offer a brief history of attempts to understand and explain leadership, followed by a summary of the qualities associated with effective school leaders.

School Administration: Leadership or Management?

A scan of book titles used in graduate education programs to prepare school administrators reveals inconsistency in what we expect of principals. Some books claim that they are about "administration"; others indicate that "leadership" is the focus. Indeed, the academic departments responsible for preparing school principals do not agree on this matter. One might be "Department of Educational Administration" whereas another uses "Department of Educational Leadership." Some confuse matters further with the term "Educational Management." Some theorists are inclined to use these terms interchangeably, but more recent literature on leadership attempts to make the distinction between the terms (Razik and Swanson 1995).

The modern word, *leader*, is derived from the Old English verb, *laeden*, which meant "to go." Today *Webster's Seventh New Collegiate Dictionary* defines the term more precisely as "to go or guide on a way, especially by going in advance." The connotation for organizations is clear: a leader sets the course for others to follow. *Administration*, on the other hand, comes to us from Latin; and in the beginning it meant "to serve." In modern contexts, administration refers to "performance of executive duties," and "to administer" means "to manage or supervise." The word *management* comes from the Latin noun *manus*, which means "hand"; and today it means, literally, "to handle" or "to control." Managers take controlling action according to instructions or procedures. Leaders, on the other hand, influence the actions of others by charting the direction of the organization.

Another aspect of leadership is important when considering the role of the principal as both a leader and a manager: the moral dimension. Leadership is a matter of moral behavior because a leader must discern the "right" course to take before influencing others to follow. History judges leaders as good or bad — which is not necessarily the same as effective or ineffective — according to what end they led their followers. For example, merely inciting a mob to riot is not a desirable end to the act of leadership. Nor is simply assessing the direction that the mob is headed, and then running to the front. Rather, leadership is turning the mob into an effective organization and then guiding that organization to do the right thing. Thomas Sergiovanni referred to leadership as having a "moral imperative" (1992, p.104).

Management is more objective. Management entails the efficient and timely accomplishment of multiple, complex tasks. It is accomplishing prescribed tasks according to established policies. Management is doing what you can with what you have.

The question for those who evaluate school principals is simple: Are we to evaluate leadership qualities or management skills? The answer, of course, is both. Razik and Swanson (1995) criticized the fashion of raising leadership to a higher level than management, as though the former is inherently more important than the other. In the effective practice of school administration, leadership and management are intertwined. The principal must be a leader of the school community. The principal also must be an efficient manager on behalf of the district office and the board of education. An evaluation system for principals must address both leadership qualities and management skills. More to the point, the evaluation system should focus on how the principal is able to integrate the two.

Approaches to Understanding Leadership and Management

The literature of ancient civilizations often contains descriptions of leadership. However, researchers did not begin to apply the methods of social science to understanding leadership until the 19th century. Short and Greer (2002, pp. 24-26) chronicled the history of modern leadership theories and identified five approaches: Great Man, trait, situational, behavioral, and contingency.

Great Man studies use biography. The method is based on the premise that careful examination of the lives of great persons will yield the personal qualities that distinguish great leaders. Howard Gardner's *Leading Minds* (1995) is such a study. While this approach makes for interesting reading, it falls short of producing a list of universal qualities.

The trait approach is similar to Great Man studies, except that the method tends to be quantitative, rather than qualitative (Short and Greer 2002). These studies also have been disappointing because the contexts for leadership differ widely. What researchers observed to be effective leadership in one circumstance did not seem to work in another.

In the behavioral approach, researchers observe how leaders are perceived by members of their groups. This approach emphasizes two aspects of leadership: consideration and initiating structure (Short and Greer 2002, p. 26). Consideration deals with how the leader relates to the members, and initiating structure deals with how the leader organizes members in order to accomplish goals.

The situational approach focuses on the characteristics of the group and the leader's response to those characteristics (Short and Greer 2002). This approach also has been disappointing. It fails to produce a universal theory of leadership because of the diversity of the groups that leaders must lead.

Finally, the contingency approach attempts to merge several of the other approaches, combining features of the behavioral and situational approaches in particular (Short and Greer 2002). Hersey, Blanchard, and Johnson (1996) used a contingency approach in developing their model for situational leadership. According to these researchers, the leader should adapt to group characteristics and group dynamics.

Standards for School Leaders

Another approach to understanding leadership can be seen in the movement toward professional standards. The Interstate School Leaders Licensure Consortium (ISLLC) of the Council of Chief State School Officers developed a set of professional standards by which school administrators should be evaluated. Most states have adopted the ISLLC Standards in some form.

The ISLLC Standards are helpful because each one is defined in terms of three dimensions: Knowledge, dispositions, and performance. They attempt to identify effective school leaders by what they know about the job, by the kind of people they are (personal attributes, values, and beliefs), and by how well they do the job. The ISLLC standards have proven useful enough that two states, Missouri and North Carolina, have created an assessment system for new superintendents based on them. Indiana, Missouri, Mississippi, North Carolina, and Ohio have designed portfolio-based assessment systems for school administrators (CCSSO 2003). ISLLC standards are listed below, and the complete document that describes the knowledge, dispositions, and performances for each standard is available on the website of the Council of Chief State Schools Officers (www.ccsso.org).

Interstate School Leaders Licensure Consortium Standards

1. A school administrator is an educational leader who promotes the success of all students by facilitating the development, articulation, implementation, and stewardship of a vision of learning that is shared and supported by the school community. (CCSSO 1996, p. 10)
2. A school administrator is an educational leader who promotes the success of all students by advocating, nurturing, and sustaining a school culture and instructional program conducive to student learning and staff professional growth. (CCSSO 1996, p. 12)
3. A school administrator is an educational leader who promotes the success of all students by ensuring management of the organizations, operations, and resources for a safe, efficient, and effective learning environment. (CCSSO 1996, p. 14)
4. A school administrator is an educational leader who promotes the success of all students by collaborating with families and community members, responding to diverse community interests and needs, and mobilizing community resources. (CCSSO 1996, p. 16)
5. A school administrator is an educational leader who promotes the success of all students by acting with integrity, fairness, and in an ethical manner. (CCSSO 1996, p. 18)

6. A school administrator is an educational leader who promotes the success of all students by understanding,
responding to, and influencing the larger political, social,
economic, legal, and cultural context. (CCSSO 1996, p.
20)

The National Association for Elementary School Principals
(2001) also has established professional standards that give guid-
ance for assessment. These standards represent a broad consensus among principals of elementary and middle schools on the
professional knowledge and skills that are vital to leading school
communities. These standards are specific in describing the form
that professional knowledge and skills should take in practice. In
*Leading Learning Communities: Standards for What Principals
Should Know and Be Able to Do* (NAESP 2001) each standard is
described in terms of the strategies that principals need to employ,
and each strategy is parsed into questions that principals can use
for self-assessment. Below are the six NAESP standards for the
principalship.

NAESP Standards for the Principalship

1. Effective leaders lead schools in a way that places student
and adult learning at the center.
2. Effective leaders set high expectations and standards for
the academic and social development of all students and
the performance of adults.
3. Effective leaders demand content and instruction that
ensures student achievement of agreed-upon academic
standards.
4. Effective leaders create a culture of continuous learning
for adults tied to student learning and other school goals.
5. Effective leaders use multiple sources of data as diagnos-
tic tools to assess, identify and apply instructional improvement.
6. Effective leaders actively engage the community to create
shared responsibility for student and school success.
(NAESP 2001, p. 2)

Despite the strides made by national organizations toward describing what school administrators need to know and be able to do, administration remains a slippery concept when we try to apply our explanations within specific contexts — that is, to very different schools in very different communities. Researchers continue to work on a unified theory that can be applied for purposes of valid and reliable evaluation.

Responsibilities, Processes, and Skills

Another way of looking at school administration comes from organizational theory. Administrators of any organization can be described in terms of three domains of behavior. The first domain comprises the responsibilities that they have as administrators. The second domain comprises the processes they use as they go about their work. And the third domain comprises the skills they need in order to be successful. Whether we realize it or not, we evaluate administrators in these terms.

Responsibility. While schools are a particular form of social institution, they have many of the basic characteristics of other modern organizations and engage in similar activities. Argyris identified the leadership activities in organizations as: 1) attainment of organizational goals, 2) maintenance of the integration of the organizational system, and 3) adaptation to forces in the organization's external environment (1964, p. 315). To these three, Sergiovanni and his colleagues (1999) added a fourth that is relevant to schools — maintaining cultural patterns.

Every administrator has four responsibilities to the organization: 1) to ensure that the organization accomplishes its mission, 2) to ensure that the internal systems work as they should so that the organization can be successful, 3) to help the organization both cope with and adapt to change, and 4) to nurture the ethos and traditions that define what is good about the school and what the school community should preserve. Of course, there is another responsibility hidden in the dynamics of these four, and that is the responsibility for achieving and maintaining balance

(Sergiovanni et al. 1999). For example, fostering change and nurturing traditions is tricky business in any organization, but especially in a school. As any school administrator knows, successfully balancing these two conflicting responsibilities, and eventually integrating them, lies at the heart of effective leadership.

Processes. Administration also is explained as a set of functions. Sergiovanni and his colleagues (1999) synthesized the work of several theorists to arrive at four functions that encompass what administrators do. First, they *lead*, guiding the subordinate members of the organization. They *organize*, creating structures for the efficient use of resources. They *plan*, setting goals and strategies for reaching goals. And finally, they *control*, reviewing personnel performance and organizational progress. All four processes must be integrated or none of them will be fully effective.

Skills. Professional skills are necessary to perform the functions of administration. Theorists continue to argue over the possible taxonomies for these skills. For the purpose of initiating a discussion on the evaluation of administrators, three broad categories are helpful: technical, interpersonal, and intrapersonal.

Making decisions, planning projects, managing finances, scheduling, and using technology are just a few of the technical skills needed in administration. Specific responsibilities will determine the actual skills needed, and those should be subject to evaluation.

Interpersonal skills focus on effective communication in both small and large groups and in one-on-one situations. Communication skills depend on good listening skills. Motivating others in an organization also is a skill, as is team-building. In surveys of teachers, the interpersonal skills of their administrators consistently are considered to be highly important.

Effective administrators also know themselves and can act on that knowledge in ways that nurture personal and professional growth (Covey 1989; Drucker 1996). They have clearly defined values, they act ethically, and they can tolerate ambiguity. These are intrapersonal characteristics. Effective administrators are self-disciplined, flexible, and adaptable to change; and they persevere in times of high stress. Goldberg (2001) identified five common characteristics among effective education leaders, four of these characteristics being intrapersonal. Effective administrators are grounded in a belief system, have the courage to stick to their beliefs — that is, to "swim upstream" (p. 758) — have a social conscience, and are devoted to their purpose. Effective administrators are optimists.

Intelligence

Intelligence is not a separate domain, but a condition for defining the aspects of effective performance. Our experience with administration would be evidence for the case of multiple intelligences. Biographies of leaders are replete with examples of "C students" who harnessed their various intelligences in particular ways.

Traditional measures of intelligence — scores on standardized tests and grade point averages — are not the issue here. However, there are certain intellectual capacities that are requisites to effective administration. First, effective administrators must have above-average cognitive ability in order to process large amounts of information quickly, allowing them to analyze different scenarios when making decisions (McShane and Von Gilnow 2003). In addition, Gardner's (1993) interpersonal and intrapersonal intelligences, echoing the preceding section, appear to be closely related to the effective practice of administration.

Personal Attributes

Effective administrators possess distinguishing personal attributes. The five common traits reported by Goldberg (2001) — bedrock beliefs, courage to swim upstream, social conscience, seriousness of purpose, and situational mastery — resonate with much of the popular literature in leadership, especially Covey's

(1989) habits of highly effective people and Drucker's (1996) observations on effective executives. Success in a public life is a matter of "personal mastery" — knowing your strengths and limitations, knowing and acting on the essence of any situation, and knowing what is most important both personally and professionally (Senge 1990). Administrators with these attributes are effective in managing others and guiding the progress of a school.

All of these personal attributes presume ethical conduct. Covey's (1991) emphasis on ethical behavior in organizations is echoed by organizational psychologists (Hogan, Curphy, and Hogan 1994). Leaders must be trustworthy. In any organization, but especially in schools, trust is earned by ethical behavior. It is lost when ethical obligations are breached.

When we apply research on leadership and management from organizational psychology and school administration, especially the work of Argyris (1964), Sergiovanni (1999), Goldberg (2001), Covey (1991), and Drucker (1996), we have a clear vision of what we should be looking for when we evaluate principals.

A Few Words About Incompetence

Sometimes we can gain a better understanding of a difficult concept by looking at its opposite. Indeed, much of our learning by experience comes from bad experiences. This also is the case with administrators. Studies from organizational psychology estimate that between 50% and 75% of administrators in organizations are incompetent (Hogan, Curphy, and Hogan 1994). There may be valuable lessons to learn from leaders who falter.

In a recent study of the characteristics of dysfunction in education organizations (O'Sullivan and Green 2003), poor leadership was identified as the primary characteristic. However, what defined "poor leadership" varied from one end of the control continuum to the other. The same observation is reported from industrial settings. Milliken-Davies (1992) found that the most common complaints about managers fell into two categories: 1) They were unwilling to exercise authority, and 2) they were over-controlling. In other words, poor leadership is found at the extremes.

Lack of trust also was found to be a key factor in dysfunctional education organizations in the study by O'Sullivan and Green (2003). Similarly, O'Sullivan and Green found that bad personnel decisions (whether in selection, retention, or promotion) can be a leading factor in changing the trajectory of an education organization, turning an effective school into one that is dysfunctional.

If we are going to evaluate principals, we need to know what we are looking for. Principals are administrators, leaders, and managers. A school community looks to the principal for vision and moral direction. At the same time, the principal is accountable for organizing and managing the resources of the school. Thus administration is a complex set of functions that can be understood as having three domains — responsibilities, processes, and skills. Responsibilities refer to attaining goals, working with internal systems so that members can work cooperatively to attain the goals, responding to changes external to the organization, and fostering the organization's identity. Processes refer to how the principal works with the school community — the style of leadership, the methods used for organizing and planning, and the degree and method of control that is exercised. Skills refer to the individual competence and expertise of the principal. Technical skills, such as scheduling and budgeting, need to be complemented by interpersonal skills, such as communicating and managing conflict. And, most important, there are intrapersonal skills, the attributes of personality and individual values and beliefs that define character. When we evaluate principals, we will be asking questions that draw from these three domains.

Chapter 3

TRADITIONAL AND EMERGING MODELS

In this chapter we will look at several models for evaluating principals. All have been applied effectively in school settings, but none is foolproof. All of them have strengths and weaknesses. The question is not which evaluation model is the best; rather, it is which evaluation model, or which combination of models, will work best for specific administrators in particular schools.

A recent analysis of practices for evaluating school administrators found a wide range of models in use (Green 2002). The use of rating scales and management by objectives were reported as most prevalent, though the frequency of using other methods is increasing. Informal evaluation remains in wide use, though just how wide is difficult to tell because "informal" evaluation often is a euphemism for "no evaluation."

In this overview, five models of formal evaluation are discussed — rating scales, management by objectives, 360-degree evaluation, professional portfolios, and assessment centers. Because it represents a different model for evaluation, the portfolio process is discussed in greater detail in Chapter Four.

Rating Scales

Rating scales remain the most popular method for evaluating principals. Their use dates back to the early 20th century, when

modern techniques of industrial management were first introduced into education. The method has endured largely because it
is so manageable. Typically, a school district will adopt a form that
lists expectations, the form will be made available to a principal,
and then the principal's immediate supervisor will complete the
form and discuss it with the principal. Many steps can be added to
elaborate this process. Principals and district administrators often
prepare a draft of the form for the board of education, which adopts
the instrument for districtwide use.

An important phase of the evaluation process using rating
scales is the pre-evaluation conference that the supervisor holds
with the principal. The supervisor discusses the form with the
principal so that there is a common understanding of each criteri-
on and what specific indicators will be used as evidence. The principal may be asked to complete a self-evaluation with the same
form so that the evaluation conference can be an opportunity for
two-way communication. After the pre-evaluation conference, the
supervisor prepares for the evaluation conference by collecting
and organizing information that is relevant to the performance
indicators. As with all personnel evaluation, the process should be
continuous.

Differences in the rating scales used in various districts have
less to do with the process than with the items listed. However,
standardization is becoming more common with the advent of
statewide requirements for principal evaluations.

The problem with rating scales, even though they remain in
wide use, is that principals do not find them especially helpful for
improving performance (Green 2002).

Management by Objectives

Management by objectives is a practice that has come from
business management. In the case of principals, management by
objectives consists of setting measurable goals at the beginning
of the evaluation period, along with incentives for reaching those
goals. At the end of the evaluation period, the principal and the

evaluator review the progress that was made toward reaching those goals.

Management by objectives has some distinct advantages. It removes subjectivity from the evaluation process. If raising the school average for standardized test scores by five percentile points is one of the objectives, there will be clear evidence at the end of the evaluation period whether that objective is met. The professional knowledge and skills that the principal will use to meet the objective are not discounted, but they are merely a means to the end. Moreover, if supplementary appropriations to the school's budget are tied to the evaluation, then the rewards system also is objective. Principals are not politicking for special favors; instead, they are focused on management objectives.

The disadvantages of management by objectives are not as obvious as the advantages, though they are no less real. It's use in business has led CEOs to concentrate on short-term goals at the expense of long-term financial strength. The same problems can occur in schools.

The problem with focusing entirely on a few intended outcomes is that we increase the likelihood of unintended outcomes. The school district that opts for management by objectives must look carefully at the systemic effects of meeting whatever goals are set. The more pressure there is to meet the objective, the more single-minded becomes the principal. This leads to a "front-burner" and "back-burner" mentality, and the tendency is to put on the front burner only those matters that will have immediate and significant effects on the short-term goal. However, education is a long-term endeavor.

The disadvantages of management by objectives should not discourage its use. But school districts should reflect carefully on the objectives that will become the focal point of the evaluation. Following is a short list of guidelines for using management by objectives.

- The objectives must be consistent with the school's mission statement.

- The level of attainment expressed in the objectives must be realistic.
- The measurements used for the objectives must be valid.
- Focused effort to meet the objectives must not produce unintended outcomes that are not consistent with the school's mission statement.
- Sufficient resources and support systems to facilitate progress toward the objectives must be available.
- The timeline for reaching the objective must allow for an appropriate planning process.
- The incentives for reaching the objective should be positive and systemic. They should benefit the entire school, not just the principal.
- The principal should participate in developing the evaluation process. There should be formal agreement to the objectives before the evaluation period begins.

Management by objectives holds great promise. Ambiguous qualities are replaced by concrete goals. The administrator's personal agenda is replaced by school and community priorities. And the process of communication between levels of administration is enhanced by the focus on what matters most. However, if the method is not implemented with care, it can result in pursuing superficial goals.

360-Degree Evaluation

The principal is a mid-level manager in a complex bureaucratic organization. At the same time, the principal is the leader of a community comprising diverse groups with their own agendas. The use of 360-degree evaluation is a response to the increasingly broad range of constituencies found in a school community. The premise of 360-degree evaluation is that information that is collected from multiple perspectives will be more valuable than information collected from only a single perspective (Dyer 2001). Researchers in the social sciences call this technique "triangulation."

The method is best understood by considering a compass. A hiker in the wilderness must traverse very difficult terrain, often without the advantage of any clear path to follow. Although the hiker has a destination in mind, it is easy to lose the course. The compass is the device the hiker uses to take bearings — to obtain reference points — in order to establish the present location and to check progress along the way. The hiker knows that the final destination is probably unattainable without the assistance of the compass. The hiker also knows that a compass is useful for finding location and charting a course only if there is more than one reference point. The more reference points there are, the more accurate will be the plot the hiker makes on the map. By frequently taking bearings with multiple reference points, the hiker will reach the destination.

When we use 360-degree evaluation, we are taking our bearings with the various constituencies of the school. The mission of the school is the destination. The feedback we collect will give us the information we need to know whether we are making progress in the right direction. We gain the information we need from different perspectives.

Effective use of 360-degree evaluation hinges on four critical issues. First, which constituencies should participate? Second, what questions should they be asked? Third, what types of instruments should be used? And fourth, how will the information be used?

Which constituencies should participate? Even though 360-degree evaluation is gaining in popularity, as yet we do not have any credible research to guide us on which sources of data are most reliable. According to Dyer (2001), the sources that are used most frequently to evaluate principals include district administrators, peers (other principals within or outside the district), parents, students, and community members not included in the other groups. Dyer also states that self-evaluation can, and should, be one of the sources. Whether any particular source is more reliable than another is disputable. Each constituent group has its own perspective, which is why we seek multiple sources of data.

The key question to consider in deciding whether to invite a group's participation is whether that group has a significant interest in what happens at the school. This clearly includes the district administrators to whom the principal reports, the teachers and auxiliary professional staff, the support staff, parents, and students.

Whether "other community members" should be included in a formal 360-degree process is debatable. First, the ambiguity of the category confuses exactly who should be asked to contribute information, thereby reducing the reliability of the data. If "community members" are to be included, the membership must be defined clearly so that the input from the group truly represents an otherwise unrepresented group.

When including peers — other principals — in the evaluation, evaluators must be cautious when using the information they report. The methods for collecting evaluation data from peers must avoid the invitation for principals to second guess each other. The process for peer input must stress the importance of principals working cooperatively with other administrators, and the instrument for collecting the data should focus on that aspect of the principalship.

What questions should be asked? While some questions will be asked of all the constituents, other questions will vary from group to group. For example, how a principal leads the faculty in the process of curriculum development will be of vital interest to teachers but of less interest to parents. Similarly, parents can be expected to provide very valuable information on how the principal communicates with the home, whereas district administrators will want to make observations on managerial expertise. Each group is in a position to make a different observation. Ideally, the 360-degree feedback forms will have a set of core questions to be answered by all the groups, then a set of special questions for each particular group.

The best way to develop the questions to ask is to involve principals and constituents themselves. For example, the creation of a set of questionnaires should begin with a steering committee, which would include subcommittees for each of the constituent groups. The steering committee should be large enough to allow the formation of a subcommittee of at least two principals and two constituents for each constituent group. Each subcommittee creates the questionnaire for that constituent group. Participants first review the responsibilities and processes that define school administration, as well as the knowledge, skills, and personal dispositions that effective principals demonstrate. At this stage, state and national standards for the principalship will be very helpful. Next, the subcommittee might review some sample forms used in other districts. Finally, the subcommittee would draft a questionnaire to be used for that group. The steering committee's job would be to format all the questionnaires to facilitate the data analysis. The Appendices include a sample questionnaire for constituent surveys.

What types of instruments should be used? Typically, questionnaires designed by the school district, with significant contribution by the district's principals, will be the method for collecting the data in a 360-degree evaluation. Commercially prepared forms also are available. As with all questionnaires, the form needs to be short and simple. If it takes longer than 10 to 15 minutes to complete, then the return rate will be low and its reliability will be diminished.

In addition to questionnaires, locally or commercially prepared standardized instruments can be very helpful in the 360-degree evaluation. Standardized instruments have many advantages. First, they provide a reference point for interpretation of data. For example, if a standardized school climate profile is used, a principal can see how the climate in his or her school compares to that of similar schools. Second, standardized instruments have undergone statistical tests for validity and reliability. The *Mental Measurements Yearbook* series is the definitive source for checking on statistical properties of various instruments. The most recent edition (Plake et al. 2003) includes instruments for measuring school climate.

Standardized instruments have a disadvantage as well. Any standardized instrument that has excellent psychometric characteristics also will be expensive to administer. In addition, persons completing a standardized form may not give it the same importance as they might give an instrument that was designed expressly for their input. An important point to remember with standardized instruments is that they should not be the sole source of data for the 360-degree evaluation. Rather, they should be merely one of the points in the triangulation process.

How shall the information be used? There are three reasons for conducting evaluations: 1) to provide data for personnel decisions; 2) to provide data to help the principal improve professional performance; and 3) to provide data to guide future professional development. Dalton (1996) argues that 360-degree evaluation data should be used only for providing the principal with feedback for professional development. Dyer (2001) states that raters will provide more reliable information if they know that the feedback process is intended for developmental purposes and is not a legally required performance evaluation.

Using 360-degree evaluation as feedback to the principal does not mean that only the principal sees the results. Dyer (2001) recommends that a coaching component accompany the 360-degree evaluation process. It is the coach, or mentor, who helps the principal interpret the data and to reflect on the conclusions so that the feedback becomes a basis for action, either for establishing goals for the school or for establishing personal goals.

Two questions emerge with the use of a 360-degree evaluation system. Who controls the data? And how will the process safeguard the confidentiality of the people who supply the data?

If the school district determines that 360-degree evaluation is to be used in conjunction with the principal's legally required performance evaluation, then the data are part of the principal's personnel file and all the safeguards that go along with personnel information must be taken. On the other hand, if the evaluation data are to be used solely for developmental purposes, then the data and any summaries of the data should belong to the principal (Dyer 2001).

A school district that implements a 360-degree evaluation system for principals must ensure that the persons who complete the questionnaires are able to do so anonymously (Dyer 2001). This means that the forms need to be administered in constituent groups large enough that there can be no speculation on which form belongs to which person.

Assessment Centers

The purpose of assessment centers is to determine a principal's strengths and to identify specific areas to be targeted for improvement. While the other evaluation methods discussed in this book examine a principal's performance in a specific school, assessment centers use simulations. The principal's performance in the simulations is evaluated by independent assessors who have been trained in the procedures and rubrics used for the assessment. The National Association of Secondary School Principals has pioneered the use of assessment centers and continues to assist schools, universities, and education service centers in establishing them (NASSP 2003).

Assessment center personnel are selected on the basis of their professional knowledge and experience. For example, at the assessment center operated by Indiana University of Pennsylvania, the assessors hold current principal certification and have been through the assessment center themselves. NASSP offers training for assessors.

Assessment by peers gives the process both credibility and reliability. Moreover, because the assessment is conducted by personnel who are not burdened by the district's politics, the assessment can be more objective.

The assessment process usually takes one day. It includes a series of simulations designed to prompt observable behaviors that are associated with effective school leadership and aligned with specific professional standards, such as the ISLLC standards (CCSSO 1996). A careful scrutiny of the activities packed into an assessment day leaves one wondering how anyone could possibly deal with such a demanding schedule, but the day is supposed to resemble what a principal really does. The following list of activities, used by an assessment center in Houston, is representative of what principals do in the assessment.

- In-basket exercises
- Group discussions
- Fact-finding exercises
- Analysis and decision-making problems
- Oral presentation exercises
- Written communication exercises

The principal is assessed according to rubrics prepared for each of the standards, giving a complete picture of the principal's professional knowledge and skills, as well as insight into the principal's values and professional ethics.

After the assessment activities, the director of the assessment center meets with the principal and reviews the results. The center's final assessment report includes a plan for professional development that is keyed to the areas identified for growth.

If a school district is using an assessment center in the selection of candidates, two issues arise. First, the school district must give candidates ample notice of the assessment and must ensure that all candidates are assessed using the same procedures. Second, the school district needs to ensure the confidentiality of all information that emerges from the assessment, just as it would any information that the candidate submits in the application process.

Research on Current Practices

Whatever evaluation model is used, it must have credibility with the principals who are being evaluated. However, rating scales remain the most prevalent form of assessment even though most principals feel that they are not helpful (Green 2002).

Principals prefer a process that uses a combination of methods. Principals report that they are more likely to value the information provided in their evaluations when it comes from multiple methods (Green 2002). In addition, principals need to be involved in the design of the process. Ownership of the process is important in establishing credibility and fairness, two necessary criteria.

Rating scales, management by objectives, 360-degree evaluation, and assessment centers all have their advantages and disadvantages. While rating scales are simple to administer, principals do not view them as helpful. Management by objectives offers a very commonsense, results-oriented approach to evaluation. However, unless the principal has a voice in setting the objectives, management by objectives can create a high-stakes, high-stress environment. While 360-degree evaluation empowers the members of the school community by inviting their observations of the principal's performance, these observations are based on limited knowledge. Thus 360-degree evaluation shows how a principal is perceived by various constituent groups, but it shows little else. And while assessment centers can provide useful information on a principal's command of processes and skills, the assessment is removed from the context of a real school.

All of these strategies and tools for evaluation have just one trait in common: They are done to the principal.

Professional portfolios, a strategy that involves the principal in the process of evaluation at every stage, from the design of the framework to the collection and interpretation of evidence to the development of a plan for professional development, is described in the next chapter.

Chapter 4

PORTFOLIOS
FOR PRINCIPALS

A principal's portfolio is a self-assessment of attributes, skills, and goals based on personal reflection and professional dialogue. It uses authentic evidence to communicate a portrait of leadership and a plan for growth. Portfolios are particularly suited for the evaluation of complex skills and elusive personal attributes.

A portfolio can be used for much more than evaluation. For example, principals' portfolios can be used for presenting experiences and qualifications to others as they compete for promotions or new positions. But the most important purpose of the principal's portfolio is to create a process for the principal's self-assessment. The portfolio is based on the premise that professional growth is an interior process that can occur only if the individual is willing to change. The will to change is spawned by self-knowledge. Whereas the other methods of evaluation begin with external observations of the principal's work, the portfolio starts with the principal's own reflection on the meaning of effective leadership in a school community and the actual evidence of that leadership.

Aspects of a Portfolio

Self-assessment. Everyone agrees that professional development is important. However, professional development should be something principals do for themselves, not something that is done to them. The first step to an effective professional development program is for principals to take control — to find out for themselves what they need to learn and how they need to change.

Principals are not too different from teachers when it comes to their performance evaluations. They are likely to become defensive if they are told about their shortcomings. But given the opportunity to identify shortcomings on their own, they are more likely to take action.

Personal reflection. Self-knowledge begins with personal reflection. The process of preparing a portfolio begins with the principal reflecting on the meaning of effective leadership in a school community. The principal must reflect on what kinds of evidence of effective leadership might be found in the school. Once a principal knows what to look for, then the process of self-assessment becomes a matter of gathering the evidence.

The gap between what a principal thinks effective leadership should look like and what evidence is actually available is the basis for setting goals. Several questions form the heart of the principal's self-assessment by personal reflection:

- What are my core values as a leader?
- What are my goals as a leader?
- Where is the evidence that the way I work reflects my core values?
- Where is the evidence that I am accomplishing my goals?
- Based on the evidence, what are my strengths and my weaknesses?
- How do my strengths and weaknesses compare to the kind of school leader I am trying to become?
- What are my professional goals, and what is my plan for working toward them?

Professional dialogue. Isolation is especially acute when principals seek meaningful dialogue on their professional practice. While many states now provide mentoring programs for beginning principals, many veteran principals still find it difficult to have a professional conversation with someone who is not in either a supervisory or subordinate role. Preparing a professional portfolio allows a principal to initiate and nurture professional dialogue on school leadership.

Principals should work in pairs or small groups when preparing and maintaining a portfolio. In this way, they can discuss what is important to communicate in the portfolio and how to communicate it.

Authentic evidence. Another key difference between a professional portfolio and other forms of professional evaluation is that the evidence in a portfolio is authentic. The self-evaluation is based on artifacts found in the school. For example, if a principal intends to document a skill in writing grants, then the abstract of a funding proposal should be included. If the principal wishes to depict a successful program to improve school climate, then a data summary from school climate surveys would be appropriate evidence. A distinctive feature of a principal's portfolio is that every statement that is made is backed up with artifacts.

Plan for growth. When principals use professional portfolios, they have a plan for professional development that is grounded in evidence that they personally gathered and interpreted. Thus they are more likely to accept individual responsibility for following through with the plan. Typically, after the principal has completed the self-assessment, the next part of the portfolio is a plan for professional development.

Creating a Principal's Portfolio

There is no standard formula for a principal's portfolio. Each one will be unique because each principal is unique and each school is unique. However, a few tips are helpful for getting started.

Organization. Typically, a principal's portfolio will be organized around a set of professional standards, such as the ISLLC or the NAESP standards, with a section devoted to each standard. The first section of the portfolio discusses personal information,

and at the end will be a section on the principal's plan for professional development.

The section on personal information should include more than
bare facts. It should provide insight into the principal's core values,
personal attributes, and professional goals. To the person reviewing the portfolio, this section will introduce what the principal
stands for as a leader. To the principal, this section is the place
where self-examination occurs on such basic matters as personal
mission. Examples of artifacts that might be included are a
résumé, a statement of the principal's philosophy of education,
results from personal assessments that describe leadership style
or decision-making style, personal awards or commendations,
and a brief biographical statement that features significant events
or people who were instrumental in shaping the principal's values
as an educator.

The next six sections — organized according to the NAESP
standards— consist of artifacts selected by the principal for their
value as evidence that the standards are met. For example, the
section for NAESP Standard Four — creating a culture of continuous learning for the adults in the school community — might
include the school's new professional development plan (or a
summary of it) that was initiated by the principal. For Standard
Five — the use of multiple sources of evidence to assess and improve instruction — the principal would include an analysis of
data from the state's and district's standardized testing programs,
with summaries of school improvement plans based on the testing. In addition, the principal might include documents that show
how teachers complement standardized tests with other assessment techniques, such as using volunteers from the business
community to assist in evaluating student portfolios. In the latter
case, a captioned photograph of a panel of business people reviewing portfolios would say a great deal about the use of alternative assessments, as well as about mobilizing community
resources. In a similar fashion, each standard should have a separate section; and each section should have a sufficient number of
artifacts to give evidence of that standard.

The last major section integrates all of the previous sections into a plan for personal development. In this section, the principal assesses strengths based on the evidence and identifies those areas that should be targeted for future growth. The plan will include a list of goals and an action plan for working on those goals. For example, a principal in a community where the predominant language of parents is Spanish might find that communication is a growing problem. The plan might suggest several goals, such as a re-evaluation of the scheme for community relations, from the school's newsletter to how the telephone is answered. Also, the principal might decide to begin a formal course of instruction in conversational Spanish. Each goal must be the result of the principal's assessment of the evidence, and each goal should be connected to a plan for growth.

Perhaps most important, the portfolio must include reflective statements. Without reflective statements, a portfolio is merely a scrapbook.

A reflective statement has several parts. First, the principal should describe what she or he is attempting to demonstrate through the evidence. Second, the statement should include a list of the artifacts that are included. And third, the principal should explain why each artifact was chosen. The last point is crucial because it makes the principal reflect on the evidence of effective leadership as it pertains to the standard. Normally, a reflective statement will be a page or two of written text, including the list of artifacts.

Format. More than a century ago, the famous American architect Louis Henri Sullivan said, "Form follows function." His observation can apply to communication as well as buildings. Thus, depending on its purpose and the type of information, the portfolio can be presented in a three-ring binder, a set of file folders, a CD, or a web page. However, the principal should remember that the purpose of the portfolio is to engage in self-assessment and professional dialogue, not just to construct a pretty package. While skill in constructing an intricate website might be valuable elsewhere, it is not the point of a portfolio. The point of the portfolio is to communicate.

The most common format of the portfolio is the three-ring binder because of the ease of updating the artifacts and the simplicity of the organization for the reviewer.

Evaluating Performance Using a Portfolio

The value of a principal's portfolio is found in the extent to which it causes the principal to engage in personal reflection, self-assessment, and professional dialogue. Accordingly, portfolios serve a function similar to professional development. They should not be the primary method by which a district evaluates principals for the purpose of personnel decisions.

Nevertheless, portfolios can be an integral part of the evaluation process. When they are used for this purpose, several important steps should be followed. First, make certain that it is the principal and not the portfolio that is being evaluated. Second, establish the purpose of the portfolio. Third, develop rubrics for the evaluation. Fourth, train the portfolio evaluators. Finally, validate the evaluation process. Without these steps, the evaluation will lose its credibility with its most important constituents — the principals.

A common error when reviewing portfolios is to be fooled by the slickness of the presentation and thus to not observe the quality of the person who is being portrayed. Evaluators will find that several questions will help them stay focused on the person, rather than on the portfolio itself.

Are the artifacts representative of the principal's initiative and leadership? All of the artifacts should be the result of the principal's own work or the work of a group that the principal directly supervised. Documents that originated from the district office or a commercial vendor are not legitimate exhibits.

Are rating scales from the principal's supervisors included? Portfolios are not intended to be a substitute for evaluation by supervisors. Rather, they should complement the supervisor's evaluation by giving it context.

Has the portfolio been professionally produced? As portfolios gain wider acceptance as a strategy for professional evaluation, professional "portfolio consultants" are becoming more common. The service is comparable to tax preparation: the principal gathers up the artifacts, and the consultant organizes the information and prepares the presentation. Often the result is a slick-looking portfolio — lots of graphics, snappy sound-bites, and eloquent reflective statements. But commercially prepared portfolios reveal only one piece of information about the principal, and that is merely how good the principal is at finding someone else to do the work. Once again, the value of the portfolio is in its personal reflection, self-assessment, and professional dialogue with peers.

Establish the Purpose of the Portfolio

The purpose of the portfolio determines the approach used in preparing it. Most will fall into one of five categories: 1) demonstrating competencies for a new position, 2) performance evaluation, 3) professional program completion, 4) evaluation for professional recognition, and 5) self-assessment.

When a principal is seeking a new position and the portfolio is going to be a means of communicating professional skills and personal attributes, the objective of the principal is to feature personal strengths. Of course, on the other side of the table, the selection committee is attempting to gain more insight into the candidate than the typical application and interview process allows and to see if there is a match between the candidate's strengths and the needs of the school.

A performance evaluation requires a different approach. In this case, specific rules and rubrics are devised, and the principal demonstrates through evidence that the evaluation criteria are met. Therefore the criteria need to be known ahead of time. The district often will have a certain number of "required exhibits."

Administrator training programs are turning to portfolios as a way to demonstrate entry-level competencies. When the purpose of a portfolio is to demonstrate competency in a set of professional standards, then even more explicit instructions on the preparation are needed. It is important for the candidate to know what kinds of evidence will be acceptable for particular standards.

Another use of portfolios is for selecting principals for professional recognition. When portfolios are being used for this purpose, both the nominees and the evaluators must know what aspects of the principalship are being emphasized in the competition and what values will be applied in the selection process.

The most common use of portfolios is professional development. The portfolio is a professional self-portrait. The portfolio becomes a mirror that reflects the progress the principal is making toward becoming the kind of school leader he or she aspires to be. Portfolios also are useful in mentoring relationships. With a mentor, the principal maps out and monitors a plan for professional growth.

Develop and Validate Rubrics

Special rubrics need to be developed if the portfolio is going to be used for performance evaluation or program completion. Probably the best example of the use of rubrics in connection with professional portfolios is the National Board for Professional Teaching Standards (NBPTS 1994), which devised a protocol for evaluating teachers for certification by the national board.

In the same manner, a district that is evaluating a principal or a university recommending a candidate for a professional certificate on the basis of a portfolio will need to create valid rubrics. When using portfolios, the validity of the evaluation process depends on the validity of the rubrics.

Evaluator Training

Whereas the validity of portfolio evaluation depends on the rubrics, the reliability will depend on the training of the evaluators. Portfolio assessment is a qualitative technique, therefore the reviewers of portfolios need training in how to interpret artifacts and how to apply the rubrics. Evaluations conducted on the basis of portfolios can be very reliable if the rubrics are valid and the evaluators have been trained in how to apply the rubrics. Typically these training sessions involve the use of simulations, where evaluators review and critique actual portfolios and compare their findings to those of other evaluators.

The professional portfolio can be a very powerful tool for evaluating principals. It has the advantage of allowing many sources of evaluative data to be included. An especially important feature is that the principal reflects on the data and uses them to devise a personal plan for professional development. Personal reflection on the meaning and evidence of school leadership, self-assessment in the context of a particular school, and professional dialogue with peers all are outcomes of the portfolio process.

Chapter 5

IMPLEMENTING AN EVALUATION SYSTEM

Peter Senge's groundbreaking work on creating the "learning organization" proposed five disciplines or "ways of knowing." The fifth discipline, which he called *systems thinking*, is the discipline that integrates the other four, which Senge identified as *personal mastery*, *mental models*, *shared vision*, and *team learning*. It is the system needed to see the big picture. It is the discipline that Senge calls the "Art of seeing the forest and the trees" (1990, p. 127). When we think about the task of evaluating principals, we want to ask, "What are the methods that we will use?" and "What effects will these methods have on all the aspects of the school system?"

School administration is a very elusive concept. James McGregor Burns (1978) observed that leadership is one of the most intensely studied phenomena on earth, but also one of the least understood. It is not a single task, nor even a simple set of tasks. An effective principal leads and manages in a complex organization with many different constituencies, multiple and sometimes conflicting goals, and bureaucratic constraints. When evaluating leadership in school communities, one size will not fit everyone. We need to design a system that will observe all the various facets of administration — responsibilities, processes, skills, and personal attributes — and allow for the integration of all these facets.

This final chapter will briefly review research on current practices, what is working and what is not. Then it discusses the steps that a school district should take in designing a system for evaluating school principals, one that sets out to help principals improve their professional practice and guide their future professional development.

Key Concepts in Designing an Evaluation System

Senge (1990) explains the essence of systems thinking in two points. First, systems have multidimensional interrelationships, rather than linear cause-effect connections. Second, systems thinking consists of seeing processes in the dimension of time, rather than seeing merely a snapshot of a moment.

These principles are important to remember when we set out to design a system for evaluating school administrators. The methods we choose and how we implement them will have many consequences throughout the school. Moreover, the methods we choose and how we implement them must be the impetus for professional growth and must help sustain that growth. Evaluation is not an event — it is a process of change.

Senge makes the distinction between "reinforcing feedback" and "balancing feedback" in explaining systems thinking (1990). This concept has valuable implications for how we evaluate principals.

Reinforcing feedback makes social organisms change their behavior, and it sustains that change. Whether we are observing an individual principal or an entire school, if we see a steady course of change, then we also will find reinforcing feedback.

Change can be desirable or undesirable. Senge (1990) refers to both "virtuous cycles" and "vicious cycles." Reinforcing feedback can make a declining situation progressively worse, or it can make an improving situation progressively better. Examples abound in school communities, from the teacher who uses positive feedback to reward responsible behavior among pupils (a "virtuous cycle") to the principal who discourages teamwork among teachers by playing favorites (a "vicious cycle"). When designing a system for the evaluation of principals, we need to ensure that we are creating a positive cycle for reinforcing feedback.

Balancing feedback is how a system corrects itself so that it reaches a goal. Riding a bicycle is an example. The rider will make adjustments in weight distribution to remain upright. However, balancing feedback can cause burnout. When expectations placed on principals, either self-imposed or top-down, are greater than the resources available to meet them (with time being the most valuable resource), these principals work longer and harder to meet those expectations. We must examine our evaluation systems to determine whether the compensating behaviors that the evaluations are producing are the kinds of behaviors we are intending to reinforce.

These key concepts in systems thinking have direct application in the evaluation of principals, and they can be restated in the form of questions.

- Does the evaluation system help supervisors to observe desirable cycles of administrator behavior?
- Does the evaluation system reinforce desirable cycles of administrator behaviors?
- Does the evaluation system have unintended consequences that are contradictory to mission of the school or the health of the organization?
- Does the evaluation system have a hidden agenda? In other words, does the system purport to evaluate one set of behaviors, but in reality a different set of behaviors is rewarded?

Grounded in systems thinking, these questions help keep the design and implementation of an evaluation system focused on the primary purposes: Improving professional performance and guiding future professional growth.

Rules of Thumb

There are six rules of thumb for designing an evaluation system for school administrators:

- Build credibility by involving the stakeholders (principals, district administrators, faculty and staff, parents) in the design.
- Establish the purpose.
- Use multiple methods.
- Ensure data are valid and reliable.
- Build in self-assessment based on personal reflection.
- Provide for continuous feedback and mentoring.

Reform and Renewal Are Inside Jobs

Today's principals are in the eye of a storm that has lasted two decades. Regrettably, all the reform initiatives that have been sprayed across the education landscape have ignored very basic principles of organizational development and personal growth.

Change is an interior process. Our schools will improve when we have better teachers and better principals. Our principals will grow as leaders when they personally reflect on the meaning of leadership in school communities and the evidence of that leadership. Evaluation should be the impetus for this personal reflection, and it should provide for the continuous feedback and mentoring that are essential for professional growth.

References

Argyris, C. *Integrating the Individual and the Organization.* New York: John Wiley, 1964.

Brown, G., and Irby, B.J. *The Principal Portfolio.* Thousand Oaks, Calif.: Corwin, 1997.

Burns, J.M. *Leadership.* New York: Harper & Row, 1978.

Clifton, D.O., and Anderson, E. *StrengthsQuest.* Washington, D.C.: Gallup Organization, 2002.

Council of Chief State School Officers (CCSSO). *Interstate School Leaders Licensure Consortium: Standards for School Leaders.* Washington, D.C., 1996.

Council of Chief State School Officers (CCSSO). "Interstate School Leaders Licensure Consortium." Retrieved 21 April 2003. www.ccsso.org/isllc.html

Covey, S.R. *Seven Habits of Highly Effective People.* New York: Simon and Shuster, 1989.

Covey, S.R. *Principle-Centered Leadership.* New York: Fireside, 1991.

Dalton, M. "Multi-Rater Feedback and Conditions for Change." *Consulting Psychology Journal: Practice and Research* 48, no. 1 (1996): 12-16.

Drucker, P. *The Effective Executive.* New York: HarperBusiness, 1996.

Dyer, K.M. "The Power of 360-Degree Feedback." *Educational Leadership* 58, no. 5 (2001): 35-38.

Farr, J.L., and Dobbins, G.H. "Effects of Self-Esteem on Leniency Bias in Self-Reports of Performance: A Structural Equation Model." *Personnel Psychology* 42 (1989): 835-50.

Gardner, H. *Frames of Mind: The Theory of Multiple Intelligences.* New York: Basic Books, 1993.

Gardner, H. *Leading Minds.* New York: Basic Books, 1995.

Genova, W.J.; Madoff, M.K.; Chin, R.; and Thomas, G.B. *Mutual Benefit Evaluation of Faculty and Administrators in Higher Education.* Cambridge, Mass.: Ballinger, 1976.

Gil, L.S. *Principal Peer Evaluation: Promoting Success from Within.* Thousand Oaks, Calif.: Corwin, 2001.

Goldberg, M. "Leadership in Education: Five Commonalities." *Phi Delta Kappan* 82 (June 2001): 757-61.

Green, J.E. "Evaluation of Administrators: Analysis of Current Practices." *Educational Leadership and Administration* 14 (2002): 113-21.

Green, J.E., and Smyser, S.O. *Teacher Portfolio: A Tool for Professional Development and Evaluation.* Lanham, Md.: Scarecrow Press, 1996.

Hersey, P.; Blanchard, K.H.; and Johnson, D.E. *Management of Organizational Behavior: Utilizing Human Resources.* Upper Saddle River, N.J.: Prentice-Hall, 1996.

Hogan, R.; Curphy, G.J.; and Hogan, J. "What We Know About Leadership: Effectiveness and Personality." In *Educational Leadership*, edited by L. Orozco. Madison, Wis.: Coursewise, 1994.

Howard, A., and Bray, D.W. "Predictions of Managerial Success Over Long Periods of Time: Lessons for the Management Progress Study." In *Measures of Leadership*, edited by K.E. Clark and M.B. Clark. West Orange, N.J.: Leadership Library of America, 1990.

Hoyt, D.P. "Evaluating Administrators." In *Designing Academic Program Reviews. New Directions for Higher Education* No. 37, edited by R.F. Wilson. San Francisco: Jossey-Bass, March 1982.

McShane, S.L., and Von Gilnow, M. *Organizational Behavior: Emerging Realities of the Workplace Revolution.* New York: McGraw-Hill, 2003.

Milliken-Davies, M. "An Exploration of Flawed First-Line Supervision." Doctoral dissertation. University of Tulsa, Okla., 1992.

National Association of Elementary School Principals (NAESP). *Leading Learning Communities: Standards for What Principals Should Know and Be Able to Do.* Alexandria, Va., 2001.

National Association of Secondary School Principals. "How to Establish a NASSP Assessment Center." 2003. www.principals.org/training/assess_info.cfm

National Board for Professional Teaching Standards (NBPTS). *Illustrative Summaries: Early Adolescence/Generalist Exercises.* Washington, D.C., 1994.

O'Sullivan, S.O., and Green, J.E. "Characteristics of Dysfunction in Educational Organizations." Paper presented to the Association for Supervision and Curriculum Development, 8 March 2003.

Plake, B.; Impara, J.; Spies, R.A.; and Pale, B.S., eds. *The Fifteenth Mental Measurements Yearbook.* Lincoln, Neb.: Buros Institute, 2003.

Razik, T.A., and Swanson, A.D. *Fundamental Concepts of Educational Leadership and Management.* Englewood Cliffs, N.J.: Prentice-Hall, 1995.

Senge, P. *The Fifth Discipline: The Art and Practice of the Learning Organization.* New York: Currency Doubleday, 1990.

Sergiovanni, T.J. *Moral Leadership.* San Francisco: Jossey-Bass, 1992.

Sergiovanni, T.J., et al. *Educational Governance and Administration* 4th ed. Boston: Allyn and Bacon, 1999.

Short, P.M., and Greer, J.T. *Leadership for Empowered Schools.* Upper Saddle River, N.J.: Merrill, Prentice-Hall, 2002.

Stine, D.O. "Developing an Evaluation System to Improve Principal Performance and Accountability." Paper presented at the annual meeting of the American Educational Research Association, Seattle, 2001.

Thomas, D.W.; Holdaway, E.A.; and Ward, K.L. "Policies and Practices Involved in the Evaluation of School Principals." *Journal of Personnel Evaluation in Education* 14, no. 3 (2000): 215-40.

Zappulla, E., ed. *Evaluating Administrative Performance: Current Trends and Practices.* Belmont, Calif.: Star, 1983.

Appendix A

SAMPLE ADMINISTRATOR EVALUATION FORM

This rating form is based on standards and rubrics for evaluating a principal's performance. It is used with permission from the Fairbanks North Star Borough School District, Fairbanks, Alaska (www.northstar.k12.ak.us).

Administrator Evaluation Form

Neither this evaluation document nor any notes, comments, or other information used in its preparation are a matter of public record.

_____	_____
Administrator	Title
_____	_____
Work Location(s)	Date
_____	_____
Evaluating Administrator	Title

Overall Evaluation Rating:
☐ Meets Standard ☐ Does Not Meet Standard ☐ Unsatisfactory

In completing this evaluation, please note:

1. *A rating of less than "meets standard" in any specific area must be explained by the evaluator in the comments section.*
2. *If the administrator's performance exceeds a standard, the evaluating administrator will provide comments in the exemplary practices section.*
3. *To determine whether a formal plan of improvement is necessary, refer to page 4 of the Administrator Evaluation Handbook.*
4. *NO/NA = not observed/not applicable.*

Standard No. 1: Leadership

1. An administrator provides leadership for an educational organization.

Overall Rating for Standard No. 1:
☐ MS   ☐ DNMS   ☐ US

Meets Standard	Does Not Meet Standard	Unsatisfactory	NO/NA
☐ Works with individuals, families, and groups to facilitate teamwork, collegiality, and professional treatment of staff.	☐ Seldom includes individuals and groups to facilitate teamwork and collegiality; professional treatment of staff is inconsistent.	☐ Teamwork and collegiality are not evident in the school; does not treat staff professionally.	
☐ Provides direction, formulates plans, and sets goals to motivate students and staff toward achieving competency.	☐ Provides inadequate direction in the formulation of plans, goal setting, and motivation of students and staff.	☐ Does not provide direction, formulate plans, or set goals to motivate students and staff toward achieving competency.	
☐ Recognizes and acknowledges outstanding performance.	☐ Does not consistently acknowledge outstanding performance.	☐ Fails to recognize outstanding performance.	
☐ Provides leadership in achieving the school's goals.	☐ Provides inconsistent leadership in achieving the school's goals.	☐ Fails to provide leadership in achieving the school's goals.	

Comments:

Exemplary Practices:

Standard No. 2: Learning Environment

2. An administrator guides instruction and supports an effective learning environment.

Overall Rating for Standard No. 2:
☐ MS   ☐ DNMS   ☐ US

Meets Standard	Does Not Meet Standard	Unsatisfactory	NO/NA
☐ Guides and supports an effective learning climate based on high expectations for students and staff.	☐ Efforts to establish a climate of high expectations for students and staff are inadequate.	☐ Does not support a climate of high expectations.	
☐ Ensures use of effective methods and facilitates effective learning environment.	☐ Efforts to guide and support the learning environment are inconsistent.	☐ Fails to guide and support the learning environment.	
☐ Maintains appropriate and accurate school records to communicate student progress.	☐ School records are incomplete, seldom used, and infrequently communicated.	☐ School records are incomplete, inaccurate, and nonexistent.	
☐ Develops and supports instructional and auxiliary programs that improve learning.	☐ Efforts to develop and support the instructional and auxiliary programs for the improvement of learning are inadequate.	☐ Instructional and auxiliary programs do not facilitate student learning.	

Comments:

Exemplary Practices:

Standard No. 3: Curriculum

3. An administrator oversees the implementation of curriculum.

Overall Rating for Standard No. 3:

☐ MS   ☐ DNMS   ☐ US

Meets Standard	Does Not Meet Standard	Unsatisfactory	NO/NA
☐ Demonstrates knowledge of current curriculum design models that include standards.	☐ Demonstrates incomplete knowledge of current curriculum models and content standards.	☐ Lacks knowledge of or disregards current curriculum and standards.	
☐ Interprets, articulates, and oversees the delivery of district curriculum at the school level.	☐ Efforts to interpret, articulate, and oversee district curriculum are inadequate.	☐ District curriculum is not followed.	
☐ Facilitates alignment of materials, curriculum, methods, goals, and standards for student performance.	☐ Inconsistently aligns materials, curriculum methods, goals, and standards for student performance.	☐ Materials, curriculum, methods, goals, and standards are not aligned.	
☐ Promotes the use of technological developments as they affect curriculum.	☐ Inconsistently promotes technological developments that affect curriculum.	☐ Fails to promote technology developments that affect curriculum.	

Comments:

Exemplary Practices:

Standard No. 4: Student Growth and Development

4. An administrator coordinates services that support student growth and development.

Overall Rating for Standard No. 4:

☐ MS   ☐ DNMS   ☐ US

Meets Standard	Does Not Meet Standard	Unsatisfactory	NO/NA
☐ Implements and oversees student behavior and discipline procedures that support student growth and development and provide for the safe and orderly atmosphere of the school.	☐ Implements and oversees behavior and discipline inconsistently or in a manner that does not support student growth and development. Attention to a safe and orderly atmosphere is inadequate.	☐ Fails to oversee discipline and behavior. Atmosphere is disorderly and unsafe.	
☐ Coordinates guidance, counseling, auxiliary, or outreach services for students.	☐ Does not consistently coordinate guidance, counseling, auxiliary, or outreach services for students.	☐ Fails to coordinate guidance, counseling, auxiliary, or outreach services for students.	
☐ Responds to family requests for information, involvement in student learning, and outreach assistance.	☐ Responds inconsistently to family requests and is inadequately involved in student learning and outreach.	☐ Discourages family requests and involvement in student learning.	
☐ Supports development and oversees implementation of comprehensive student activities that connect schooling with life.	☐ Activities that connect school to life are minimal or have not been implemented.	☐ No evidence that connections between school and life are promoted.	

Comments:

Exemplary Practices:

Standard No. 5: Staffing and Professional Development

5. An administrator provides staffing and professional development to meet student learning needs.

Overall Rating for Standard No. 5:
☐ MS   ☐ DNMS   ☐ US

Meets Standard	Does Not Meet Standard	Unsatisfactory	NO/NA
☐ Supervises staff to improve their performance; uses both collegial and hierarchical models, as appropriate.	☐ Supervision is inconsistent.	☐ Supervision is ineffective.	
☐ Works with staff to identify individual and group professional needs; designs appropriate staff development opportunities.	☐ Planning for staff development is not aligned with the needs of the staff and the district.	☐ Staff development is poorly planned or not emphasized.	
☐ Evaluates staff in a timely manner for the purpose of making recommendations about retention, and evaluations reflect high expectations for continued professional development.	☐ Evaluations of staff for purposes of retention are inconsistent or untimely.	☐ Evaluation of staff is ineffective.	
☐ Coordinates the hiring of staff based on student learning needs.	☐ Inconsistent efforts to hire staff based on student learning needs.	☐ Ineffective efforts to hire staff based on student learning needs.	

Comments:

Exemplary Practices:

Standard No. 6: Assessment and Evaluation

6. An administrator uses assessment and evaluation information about students, staff, and the community in making decisions.

Overall Rating for Standard No. 6:
☐ MS   ☐ DNMS   ☐ US

Meets Standard	Does Not Meet Standard	Unsatisfactory	NO/NA
☐ Uses district or state adopted tools and develops effective processes to gather information to meet program goals.	☐ Processes used to gather information are unreliable or ineffective.	☐ Processes are not used to gather information.	
☐ Uses information to evaluate student, school, and program goals, and implements change where appropriate.	☐ Does not consistently use information to evaluate student, school, and program goals.	☐ Misinterprets or fails to use information to evaluate student, school, and program goals.	

Comments:

Exemplary Practices:

Standard No. 7: Curriculum

7. An administrator communicates with diverse groups and individuals with clarity and sensitivity.

Overall Rating for Standard No. 7:
□ MS   □ DNMS   □ US

Meets Standard	Does Not Meet Standard	Unsatisfactory	NO/NA
□ Communicates and uses feedback with clarity, effectiveness, and sensitivity within the school and community.	□ Communication is unclear, ineffective, or insensitive to the needs of others; feedback is misinterpreted.	□ Communication and feedback are counterproductive to the educational process.	
□ Communicates a positive image of the school in the community and recognizes the influence of culture on communication.	□ Does not effectively communicate a positive image of the school; inconsistently demonstrates sensitivity to cultural influences.	□ Image of the school is negative, and there is a lack of sensitivity to community and cultural influences.	
□ Treats students and adults with respect.	□ Insufficient respect shown to students or adults.	□ Interaction with students or adults is negative, demeaning, sarcastic, or disrespectful.	
□ Is open to family comments and is responsive to family concerns.	□ Responds inconsistently to family concerns.	□ Family concerns are disregarded.	

Comments:

Exemplary Practices:

Standard No. 8: Laws, Policies, Procedures, and Good Business Practice

8. An administrator acts in accordance with established laws, policies, procedures, and good business practice.

Overall Rating for Standard No. 8:
□ MS   □ DNMS   □ US

Meets Standard	Does Not Meet Standard	Unsatisfactory	NO/NA
□ Administers and acts in accordance with federal and state laws and district policies.	□ Lacks knowledge of and acts inconsistently with regard to federal and state laws or district policies.	□ Does not comply with federal and state laws or district policies.	
□ Administers contracts and financial accounts responsibly, accurately, and effectively.	□ Efforts to administer contracts and financial accounts are ineffective, inconsistent, or inaccurate.	□ Does not administer contracts and financial accounts.	

Comments:

Exemplary Practices:

Standard No. 9: Social, Cultural, Political, and Economic Forces

Overall Rating for Standard No. 9:
☐ MS   ☐ DNMS   ☐ US

9. An administrator understands the influence of social, cultural, political, and economic forces on the educational environment and uses this knowledge to serve the needs of children, families, and communities.

Meets Standard	Does Not Meet Standard	Unsatisfactory	NO/NA
☐ Actions reflect awareness of relationships between policy and education; supports efforts to promote quality education.	☐ Actions reflect lack of awareness of relationships between policy and education; inconsistently supports quality education.	☐ Denies the relationship between policy and education; fails to support quality education efforts.	
☐ Recognizes the appropriate level at which issues should be resolved and consistently takes necessary action.	☐ Fails to recognize the level at which issues should be resolved; actions are ineffective.	☐ Problems are not resolved at the appropriate level or actions taken are detrimental.	
☐ Addresses ethical practices, acting with care and judgment and within appropriate time lines.	☐ Inconsistently or reluctantly addresses ethical practices or does not meet appropriate time lines.	☐ Fails to address ethical practices or does not act with care or judgment.	

Comments:

Exemplary Practices:

Standard No. 10: Parents and Families

Overall Rating for Standard No. 10:
☐ MS   ☐ DNMS   ☐ US

10. An administrator facilitates the participation of parents and families as partners in the education of children.

Meets Standard	Does Not Meet Standard	Unsatisfactory	NO/NA
☐ Supports and respects the variety of positive parenting traditions and practices; respects and supports parent and family participation.	☐ Support and respect of positive parenting traditions and practices is inconsistent; fails to encourage parent and family participation.	☐ Positive parenting traditions and practices are not recognized.	
☐ Ensures that teachers provide opportunities to engage families to assist in student learning.	☐ Does not ensure that teachers and staff provide opportunities to engage families to assist in student learning.	☐ Does not recognize the value of engaging families in student learning.	
☐ Involves parents and community in meaningful decision making that maintains school programs.	☐ Inconsistently involves parents and community in meaningful decision making and in the maintenance of school programs.	☐ Fails to involve parents and community in decision making and in the maintenance of school programs.	
☐ Provides information to families in a timely manner to facilitate meaningful participation.	☐ Information provided to families is not timely and does not facilitate participation.	☐ Fails to provide information to families.	
☐ Maintains a school climate that welcomes families.	☐ Does not maintain a school climate that welcomes families.	☐ School climate discourages family participation.	

Comments:

Exemplary Practices:

Evaluating Administrator's Signature: _____

Date: _____

Administrator's Signature*: _____

Date: _____

* Signature does not constitute endorsement of the evaluation, but indicates the evaluation has been read and discussed. Additional sheets may be attached by the evaluator or the evaluatee who desires to make a comment.

Appendix B

SURVEY FORMS
FOR 360-DEGREE
EVALUATION

The following forms are used to obtain community input for evaluating principals. The first form is used with parents and other community members, and the second is used with teachers. They are used with permission from the Fairbanks North Star Borough School District, Fairbanks, Alaska (www.northstar. k12.ak.us).

Parent/Other Input Form for Building Administrator

Neither this input document nor any notes, comments, or other information used in its preparation are a matter of public record.

_____   _____
Building Administrator   Date

_____
School
      ☐ Elementary   ☐ Secondary   ☐ Secondary Assistant

☒ *An "agree" rating indicates that administrator meets each listed standard in a category.*

☒ *Please explain any rating of "disagree" in the comments section.*

☒ *Mark NO/NA if not observed or not applicable.*

Building administrator meets the standard:

Standard A: Provides leadership for our school.   Agree   Disagree   NO/NA

Works with parents, staff, and students in developing a   ☐   ☐   ☐
school vision and promoting it. Implements the plan of
action to achieve goals. Seeks solutions to problems and
appropriately responds to concerns.

Comments:

Standard B: Guides instruction and supports an effective   Agree   Disagree   NO/NA
learning environment.

Has high expectations for the performance of students and staff.   ☐   ☐   ☐
Develops and supports programs that improve learning. Ensures
that facilities are safe, clean, orderly, and well maintained.

Comments:

Standard C: Oversees the implementation of curriculum.   Agree   Disagree   NO/NA

Ensures effective delivery of course content. Monitors student   ☐   ☐   ☐
grading policy. Promotes the use of technological developments.

Comments:

Standard D: Coordinates services that support student   Agree   Disagree   NO/NA
growth and development.

Effectively coordinates programs that promote student   ☐   ☐   ☐
safety, growth, and responsibility, including counseling,
special services, and student activities. Administers student
discipline fairly and consistently. Acts to ensure safety of
students, personnel, and school property.

Comments:

Standard E: Provides for staffing and professional   Agree   Disagree   NO/NA
development to meet student learning needs.

Effectively supervises staff. Makes staff assignments based   ☐   ☐   ☐
on student learning needs.

Comments:

Standard F: Uses assessment and evaluation information   Agree   Disagree   NO/NA
about students, staff, and the community in making
decisions.

Uses assessment information on student, school, and program   ☐   ☐   ☐
performance to implement change where appropriate. Ensures
that student progress is monitored and reported to parents in a
clear and timely fashion.

Comments:

Standard G: Communicates with diverse groups and   Agree   Disagree   NO/NA
individuals with clarity and sensitivity.

Communicates effectively with the school community. Treats   ☐   ☐   ☐
students and adults with respect. Is open to parent comments
and is responsive to parent concerns.

Comments:

Standard H: Acts in accordance with established laws,   Agree   Disagree   NO/NA
policies, procedures, and good business practices.

Complies with established laws, policies, procedures, and   ☐   ☐   ☐
good business practices.

Comments:

Standard I: Understands the influence of social, cultural, political, and economic forces on the educational environment and uses this knowledge to serve the needs of children, families, and communities.	**Agree**	**Disagree**	**NO/NA**
Acts with an understanding of social, racial, cultural, political, and economic forces that influence a positive school environment.	☐	☐	☐

Comments:

Standard J: Facilitates the participation of parents and partners in the education of their children.	**Agree**	**Disagree**	**NO/NA**
Maintains a school climate that welcomes parents and families and invites their participation. Ensures that teachers provide opportunities to engage families to assist in student learning. Involves parents and community in meaningful decision making. Provides information to families in a timely manner to facilitate meaningful participation.	☐	☐	☐

Comments:

General comments (additional comment page may be attached):

_____   _____
Name (please print)   Telephone

_____   _____
Signature   Date

Teacher Input Form for Building Administrator

Neither this input document nor any notes, comments, or other information used in its preparation are a matter of public record.

_____   _____
Building Administrator   Date

_____   _____
Work Location(s)   Teacher

☐ Elementary   ☐ Secondary   ☐ Secondary Assistant

X An "agree" rating indicates that administrator meets each listed standard in a category.

X Any rating of "disagree" must be explained in the comments section, and concerns shall have been previously brought to the attention of the building administrator.

X Mark NO/NA if not observed or not applicable.

	Building administrator meets the standard:		
Standard A: Leadership	**Agree**	**Disagree**	**NO/NA**
Promotes shared vision with individuals and groups, facilitates teamwork and collegiality. Formulates goals, establishes priorities, and develops action plans to accomplish the school's mission. Provides leadership in expectations of high student achievement and communicates effective instructional methods.	☐	☐	☐
Comments:			
Standard B: Curriculum	**Agree**	**Disagree**	**NO/NA**
Knows, understands, and facilitates aligned standards-based curriculum, methods, and technology. Successfully implements assessment policy.	☐	☐	☐
Comments:			
Standard C: Support and Safety	**Agree**	**Disagree**	**NO/NA**
Coordinates programs and services that promote student safety, growth, development, and responsibility. Acts to ensure safety and security of students, personnel, and school property within the school facility, on school grounds, and in school-related activities off school property.	☐	☐	☐
Comments:			
Standard D: Staffing	**Agree**	**Disagree**	**NO/NA**
Coordinates the interview and selection process to identify and recommend quality personnel for hire. Assigns staff appropriately.	☐	☐	☐
Comments:			
Standard E: Professional Development	**Agree**	**Disagree**	**NO/NA**
Supervises and evaluates staff through a positive process designed to improve skills, instructional programs, and	☐	☐	☐

support services. Provides opportunities for professional development. Motivates staff to participate in professional development.

Comments:

Standard F: Communication	Agree	Disagree	NO/NA
Recognizes and uses varied methods to communicate effectively with the school community and local media.	☐	☐	☐

Comments:

Standard G: Laws, Policies, Procedures, and Good Business Practice	Agree	Disagree	NO/NA
Administers and acts in accordance with federal and state laws, board policies, and regulations. Works within district policies, procedures, and directives. Administers school's budget, financial accounts, and contracts consistent with district procedures and in a responsible, accurate, and effective manner. Knows, understands, and acts in accordance with process required for district's compliance with special education and civil rights laws and regulations. Knows, understands, and acts in accordance with the terms of negotiated agreements for certified and classified employees. Administers student discipline according to district policies and regulations in a fair and consistent manner.	☐	☐	☐

Comments:

Standard H: Social, Cultural, Political, and Economic Factors	Agree	Disagree	NO/NA
Recognizes and acts with understanding of the social, racial, cultural, political, and economic forces that influence a positive school environment.	☐	☐	☐

Comments:

Standard I: Parents and Community	Agree	Disagree	NO/NA
Actively seeks the involvement of diverse family and community members in all facets of the school program. Provides a supportive and respectful school environment. Encourages volunteer participation of parents and community members.	☐	☐	☐

Comments:

Standard J: Facilities Maintenance and Operation	Agree	Disagree	NO/NA
Ensures that facilities are safe, clean, orderly, and well maintained.	☐	☐	☐

Comments:

General comments (additional comment page may be attached):

_____   _____
Teacher's Signature   Date

_____   _____
Building Administrator's Signature*   Date

*Signature does not necessarily indicate agreement with input.

Appendix C

GOAL-DIRECTED EVALUATION FORM

The following form provides an example of a goal-directed evaluation process. It is used with permission from the Fairbanks North Star Borough School District, Fairbanks, Alaska (www. northstar.k12.ak.us).

Professional Goal Setting Evaluation Instrument for Administrators

Neither this evaluation document nor any notes, comments, or other information used in its preparation are a matter of public record.

_____   _____
School Administrator   Work Location

_____   _____
Evaluating Administrator   Title

_____
Observation Date/Time

Ratings: MS = Meets Standard   DNMS = Does Not Meet Standard

School administrator meets the following district standards:	MS	DNMS
1. Leadership	☐	☐
2. Learning Environment	☐	☐
3. Curriculum	☐	☐
4. Student Growth and Development	☐	☐
5. Staffing and Professional Development	☐	☐
6. Assessment and Evaluation	☐	☐
7. Communication	☐	☐
8. Established Laws, Policies, Procedures, and Good Business Practice	☐	☐
9. Social, Cultural, Political, and Economic Forces	☐	☐
10. Parents and Families	☐	☐

School administrator understands and complies with the following:	MS	DNMS
1. Alaska school laws and regulations	☐	☐
2. District and building administrative directives	☐	☐
3. Building policies/handbook	☐	☐
4. Curriculum guides	☐	☐
5. Negotiated agreements	☐	☐
6. Alaska Department of Education rules and regulations	☐	☐
7. School Board policies and administrative regulations	☐	☐
8. Administrator Evaluation Handbook	☐	☐
9. PTPC Code of Ethics	☐	☐

_____   _____

Evaluating Administrator's Signature   Date

_____   _____

School Administrator's Signature   Date

Professional Goals for the Current Year

Data Reflection

One Professional Leadership Goal. *Based on reflection or input from these and other sources, chose one professional leadership goal you wish to focus upon for the year.*

- Complete the School Leadership Self-Inventory. To be done at a meeting in the fall after school gets under way.
- Identify strengths and personal needs.
- Review goals.
- Review teacher input forms.
- Review climate survey.
- Review summaries of student assessment data.

District Focus Goals for the School Year

- Student Achievement
- Parent Involvement Programs

---

1. List the Professional Leadership Goal you plan to focus on this year. The goal should facilitate the learning process and/or professional leadership skills. Goals must be based on school board goals and the district's administrative standards. Write two (2) easily measurable and verifiable objectives for the goal.

2. List the Student Achievement Goal you plan to focus on this year. This goal should reflect your role in increasing student achievement in your school. Write two (2) easily measurable and verifiable objectives for the goal.

3. List one goal for how you plan to implement the Parent Involvement Policy in your school this year. Write two (2) easily measurable and verifiable objectives for the goal.

(to be completed by May 1)

1. Was the plan completed?   ☐ Yes   ☐ No

Comments by School Administrator:

Comments by Assistant Superintendent:

2. Will the plan be continued next year?   ☐ Yes   ☐ No

3. Will modifications be made?   ☐ Yes   ☐ No

If so, indicate modifications below:

_____   _____
Assistant Superintendent's Signature   Date

_____   _____
School Administrator's Signature*   Date

*Signature does not constitute endorsement of the evaluation.

Appendix D

SAMPLE PORTFOLIO

This list of elements in a portfolio is based on the Interstate School Leaders Licensing Consortium's *Standards for School Leaders*. Because each school and principal have different situations, the actual items in the portfolio will differ.

There is no rule on how many artifacts are needed. However, it is important to include some form of evidence for each standard. In addition, the section for each standard should include a reflective statement on the meaning of that standard and how the evidence that is presented supports that standard.

Sample Organization of Artifacts for a Principal's Portfolio

I. **Personal Introduction**
- Résumé.
- Brief autobiography, with emphasis on role models and mentors.
- Personal reflection on the role of the principal.
- Scrapbook page of photographs, with captions, showing family and personal interests.

II. **Standard 1: Educational Vision**
- Personal statement interpreting this standard, along with an explanation of how these artifacts serve as evidence of this standard.
- Copy of school's strategic plan, with brief outline of the process used for consensus building.
- Video of an oral presentation to PTA explaining strategic plan.
- Case study illustrating how systems theory was used to solve a chronic problem, such as tardiness after lunch periods.

III. **Standard 2: Instructional Leadership**
- Personal statement interpreting this standard, along with an explanation of how these artifacts serve as evidence of this standard.

- Graph showing trend lines for improvement in state test scores.
- School improvement plan, with outline of the process used for building consensus.
- Procedures for involving faculty in teacher interviewing process.
- Professional development plan for the school, with brief outline of the process used to create the plan.
- Brochure describing online homework center created in collaboration with student council and PTA.
- Student handbook for academic mentoring program.
- Program evaluation for student conflict resolution program.
- Excerpts from minutes from curriculum committee meetings, with attached explanation of the curriculum alignment project.

IV. Standard 3: School Management
- Personal statement interpreting this standard, along with an explanation of how these artifacts serve as evidence of this standard.
- Graph showing trend lines for increase in portion of budget directed to student development and faculty development.
- Graph showing trend lines for decrease in accidents on campus.
- Table depicting organization of departments following restructuring project, with brief outline of the process used for building consensus.
- Operational plan for use of temporary classrooms during renovation.
- Operational plan for implementing an integrated system for data management.

V. Standard 4: Community Leadership
- Personal statement interpreting this standard, along with an explanation of how these artifacts serve as evidence of this standard.
- Scrapbook page of photographs, with captions, showing local companies participating in career fair.
- Scrapbook page of photographs, with captions, showing student community projects.
- Executive summary of goals and accomplishments of the school site council.
- Executive summary of grant from Chamber of Commerce to implement "Community-to-Student Mentoring Program."
- Executive summary of grant from Rotary Club to implement community oral history project.
- Copy of school newsletter (English edition, Spanish edition, and Korean edition).
- Letter of appreciation for services as chair of voter registration committee.

VI. Standard 5: Ethical Leadership
- Personal statement interpreting this standard, along with an explanation of how these artifacts serve as evidence of this standard.
- Case study depicting an ethical dilemma and how it was resolved.
- Statement of personal values used for making professional decisions.
- Personal mission statement.

VII. Standard 6: Political Leadership
  • Personal statement interpreting this standard, along with an explanation of how these artifacts serve as evidence of this standard.
  • Letter showing office held in the state principals association.
  • Program showing participation as a panelist in a local forum on education reform hosted by the local university.
  • PowerPoint notes from a presentation given on education reform to a local Kiwanis Club.
  • Copy of op-ed article on public education that was published in local newspaper.

VIII. Professional Development Plan
  • Personal analysis of strengths.
  • Summary of evaluations by superintendent from past three years.
  • Personal analysis of survey of parents on professional performance.
  • Statement of personal professional goals, with strategies for accomplishing those goals.
  • Copy of letter indicating approval of doctoral dissertation proposal.
  • List of workshops and clinics planned for attendance in next year, cross-referenced with professional goals.